Atsuko Morozumi's

Contents

Join-in Stories for the Very Young

Stories by Mathew Price
Illustrations by Atsuko Morozumi

MATHEW PRICE LIMITED

Hardback edition: ISBN 1-84248-000-6
Paperback edition: ISBN 1-84248-102-9

Paperback edition first published 2003 by Mathew Price Limited
Hardback edition first published 2000 by Mathew Price Limited
The Old Glove Factory, Bristol Road, Sherborne, Dorset DT9 4HP
Manufactured in China

Will You Be My Friend?

Little chicks are usually born with lots of brothers and sisters, but there was one little chick who was born all alone.

And he was lonely.

'I'm lonely,' he said to his father, the rooster, 'Will you play a game with me?'

'Not just now,' said father, 'I have to practise my alarm call. Why don't you find a friend?'

So the little chick went
to see the farm dog.
'Will you be my friend?'
he asked him.

'Not now,' said the dog.
'I'm busy.'

'Doing what?' asked the
chick.

'Guard duty, of course,'
said the dog. 'Why
don't you ask the cat?'

So the little chick went to see the cat.
'I'm all alone in the world and I need a friend,' said the little chick. 'Will you be my friend?'

'Not now,' said the cat. 'I'm busy.'

'What are you doing?' asked the chick.

'Hunting,' said the cat.

'Hunting what?' said the chick.

'Rats, of course,' said the cat. 'Now leave me alone. Ask the Old Goat.'

The Old Goat was munching hay at the back of the barn. 'Old goat,' asked the little chick, 'Will you be my friend? Or are you too busy as well?'

'Busy?' said the Old Goat, 'Hmmm. Not too busy. Just let me finish this hay.'

'Well, who can I play with?' said the little chick.

At that moment a big red fox jumped out of the hedge beside him.

'Play with me,' he said. And he grabbed the little chick in his mouth and galloped off towards his den.

'COCKADOODLEDO!
A fox! A fox! A fox!'

When the dog, the cat, the
cows, the pigs, the ducks
and Old Goat heard the
alarm, they all stopped
what they were doing and
ran after the fox.

When the fox saw all the animals chasing after him, he dropped the little chick and ran for his life.

And he never came back.

After that the little chick found he had lots of friends – and sometimes they were not too busy to play a game with him.

THE END

Bears Don't Swim

It was a beautiful summer's day. Bear was in his hammock
when his friends called to see him on their way to the beach.
'It's a great day for a swim, Bear. Are you coming?' they said.
'No, no,' said Bear. 'Bears don't swim.'

'We've got honey sandwiches,' they said.

'Honey sandwiches!' said Bear.

'I'll get my bike,' he said.

Bear didn't care where he went, as long as there were honey sandwiches when he got there. So they all set off for the beach.

When they got there, Bear spread his rug on the top of the
sand dunes and settled down to eat the sandwiches.

'I do love honey sandwiches,' said Bear.

'But *why* do they go so fast?' And he sighed.

And fell asleep.

His friends were having a wonderful time on the beach below. They never noticed Bear roll over in his sleep . . . and over and over . . .

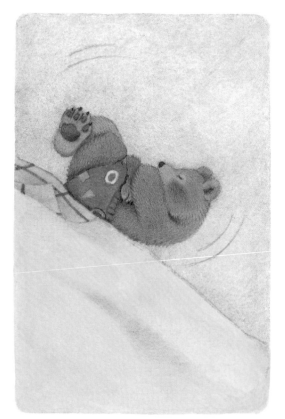

and over . . .

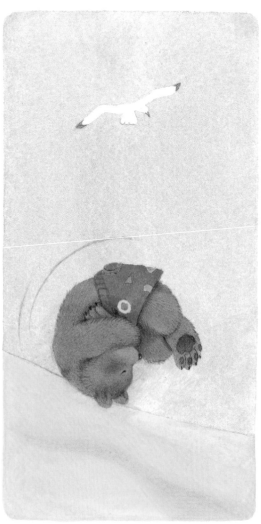

and over . . .

until suddenly . . .

KERSPLASH!

'Help!' he called.

'I can't swim!'

'Bears don't . . .

'Wait a minute . . .

'I've changed my mind.

'Bears do swim!'

And swim he did. Bear found out that he loved swimming
as much as – well, as much as honey sandwiches.

So he swam,   and played,   all day long.

He was still swimming long after it was time to go home.

After that, Bear swam as often as he could. When the winter came, he went to the swimming baths and swam there. 'I never knew,' he said, 'that bears could swim.'

THE END

Picture Stories

This is a series of pictures with so much happening
in them that you can make up your own stories

Wind

Rain

Snow

Sun

THE END

The Old Alligator

This is an action story
with instructions for joining in

THREE little ducks were playing in the river,

When along came an alligator, looking for his dinner.

(Make looking sign, with hand shading eyes as if searching the horizon for dinner)

The old alligator went SNAP! SNAP! SNAP! (Clap, Clap, Clap)

And TWO little ducks were left.

Two little ducks were swimming for their lives,

But the old alligator gave a great big smile. (Pull sides of mouth wide)

The old alligator went SNAP! SNAP! SNAP! (Clap, Clap, Clap)

And ONE little duck was left.

ONE little duck was trying to reach the bank, *(Make paddling motions with hands)*

But the old alligator was much too fast.

The old alligator went SNAP! SNAP! SNAP!   (Clap, Clap, Clap)

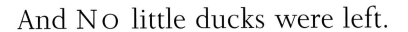

And NO little ducks were left.

The old alligator climbed up the bank with
THREE little ducks inside. *(Rub tummy with circular motion)*

A baby elephant, passing by, stumbled on the alligator, squashing him flat. *(Put hands flat on floor)*

Out popped the little ducks, POP! POP! POP! (Clap, Clap, Clap)

And scampered back to Mummy as fast as they could go.

'Oops', said the elephant, 'sorry old man.'

But that old alligator was FLAT! FLAT! FLAT! (Slap the floor with palms three times)

THE END

Go Away, Mr Wolf!

Knock!
Knock!
Knock!
Who's that knocking at our
little front door?

'Anyone for ice cream?' said a furry, friendly voice.

Knock!
Knock!
Knock!
Who's that knocking at our
little front door?

'Coming for a drive?'
said a charming,
cheery voice.

Knock! Knock! Knock!
Who's that knocking at our
little front door?

'Anyone for a game?' said a hoarse but hopeful voice.

Knock!
Knock!
Knock!
Who's that knocking at our
little front door?

'It's a lovely day
for a swim.
Anybody coming
with me?'

Knock!
Knock!
Knock!
Who's that knocking at
our little front door?

'Anybody home?'

THE END